I0796990

FOR MY BEST FRIEND, DOLLY —F.E.

ILLUSTRATED BY

ALISSA LEVY

WRITTEN & EDITED BY FRANCES EVANS

DESIGNED BY ZOE BRADLEY

COVER DESIGN BY JOHN BIGWOOD

UNION SQUARE & CO. and the distinctive Union Square & Co. logo are trademarks of Sterling Publishing Co., Inc.

Union Square & Co., LLC, is a subsidiary of Sterling Publishing Co., Inc.

First published in Great Britain in 2024 by LOM ART, an imprint of
Michael O'Mara Books Limited, 9 Lion Yard, Tremadoc Road, London SW4 7NQ

Published by Union Square & Co. in 2025.

ISBN 978-1-4549-6089-8

For information about custom editions, special sales, and premium purchases, please contact specialsales@unionsquareandco.com.

Printed in China

2 4 6 8 10 9 7 5 3 1

unionsquareandco.com

Dogs ARE A WOMAN'S BEST FRIEND

UNION SQUARE & CO.
NEW YORK

CONTENTS

WOMAN'S BEST FRIEND

If you've picked up this book, chances are you don't need to be told just how incredible dogs are. You might even be snuggled on the sofa with your own furry best friend right now. From teeny Chihuahuas to giant Great Danes, dogs bring joy, fun, and friendship to millions of people around the world.

This book celebrates the unique and deeply special bond between 30 amazing women and their equally paw-some pooch pals. Artists, scientists, activists, and world leaders—discover the stories of inspiring women past and present and the dogs who have stood faithfully beside them.

Dogs are truly remarkable creatures, and the bond they share with us is unlike that of any other animal. Dogs can read our faces, follow our hand gestures, and seem to have a built-in superpower to sense our moods. As well as being beloved companions, dogs work alongside us; service dogs help to keep us safe, assistance dogs support us, and therapy dogs bring us comfort.

They are also our oldest animal friends. All dogs are descended from ancient wolves, which were the first animals to be domesticated by humans at least 15,000 years ago. Some scientific studies have suggested that it was the bond between women and their dogs that cemented this relationship and was instrumental in making dogs not just a hunting companion, but one of the family.

As well as taking inspiration from the stories in this book, you can learn lessons for life from a dog's perspective, discover some record-breaking canines in the Hall of Fame, and take a test to find your paw-fect doggie match.

Marilyn Monroe famously sang that "diamonds are a girl's best friend." But who needs diamonds when you've got a dog?

OPRAH WINFREY

— TV HOST, PRODUCER & AUTHOR —

Well-known for her love of canine companions, Oprah Winfrey has had more than 20 dogs over the years. She currently has three: Sadie the cocker spaniel and two springer spaniels called Sunny and Lauren, all of whom were adopted from a Chicago-based shelter, PAWS.

Oprah says nothing makes her happier than being with her dogs and describes them as her fur children. What could be more comforting than having a furry friend resting by your feet while you read a good book?

An honest and engaging personality has earned Oprah world-famous status. She hosted *The Oprah Winfrey Show* for 25 seasons, transforming a previously faltering talk show into the highest-rated television talk show in the United States, winning several Emmy Awards.

"For me, a home without dogs would be like a library without books."

Since the last episode aired in 2011, Oprah has worked on many other projects, including her groundbreaking book club, which started as a television segment on her show but is still running today.

Oprah has put her hand to many things, including acting, producing, and writing self-help books. She has also been involved in many philanthropic activities, raising awareness of inequality and creating her own charity, Oprah's Angel Network. This philanthropic streak is extended into canine territory, as her three current dogs are all rescue dogs who were at risk of being euthanized if they hadn't been rehomed. Now, they are estimated to inherit 30 million dollars. What a twist of fate.

ARIANA GRANDE

SINGER-SONGWRITER & ACTOR

Pop megastar Ariana Grande began singing and acting as a child before getting her big break on Nickelodeon in 2009. After a stratospheric rise that has seen Ariana pick up Grammys and smash world records, she has become one of the best-selling music artists of all time. Ariana quietly shares the profits of her success with charities that are important to her. She is passionate about animal rights, and dogs in particular hold a special place in her heart.

Ariana has almost as many dogs as music awards. Ariana has adopted all her dogs from rescue centers and uses her superstar status to promote the importance of giving animals who have had a tough start a loving fur-ever home. Her cherished pack includes a bloodhound called Lafayette, a pitbull mix called Myron, and a Yorkshire terrier called Strauss.

One of her most constant canine companions is a Chihuahua-beagle cross called Toulouse. He was rescued by Ariana in 2013 and was named after the orange-colored kitten in the Disney film *The Aristocats.*

Little Toulouse is never far from Ariana's side and often accompanies her on tour, providing joy and comfort when she's not performing. Toulouse himself is no stranger to the limelight, regularly popping up on Ariana's social media accounts and appearing in music videos, adverts, and even on the cover of *Vogue*.

> **"Dogs are the most harmless, sweetest babes in the world. They show nothing but unconditional love, so they deserve that in return."**

CLEOPATRA

PHARAOH

A trailblazing leader, a gifted scholar, a romantic icon . . . and a dog lover. While Cleopatra's relationships with Julius Caesar and Mark Antony have become the stuff of legend, less well-known is her passion for her four-legged friends.

These noble dogs were the perfect match for Egypt's discerning queen.

Cleopatra was born circa 69 BCE and became queen of Egypt when she was just 18 years old. In an era when Egypt's female rulers were largely unheard of in the wider world, Cleopatra gained international fame for her diplomatic skills, political reforms, and intellect. A talented linguist, she could speak multiple languages, including Greek, Egyptian, Latin, and Ethiopian, and her court in Alexandria was a haven for philosophers, scientists, and artists.

Her court was probably home to quite a few dogs, too. Like many ancient Egyptians, Cleopatra is thought to have had a soft spot for hounds—she is said to have owned several and presented her lover Julius Caesar with a gift of puppies in 48 BCE.

The ancestors of modern-day greyhounds, ancient Egyptian dogs were prized for their companionship and hunting skills. They were so beloved that when a pet pooch passed away, it would be laid to rest in its human family's tomb in the hope that owner and dog would be reunited in the afterlife. Powerful yet elegant, gentle yet fiercely loyal, these noble dogs were the perfect match for Egypt's discerning queen.

HEDY LAMARR

ACTOR & INVENTOR

Dubbed the "world's most beautiful woman," actor Hedy Lamarr was the toast of Hollywood in the 1930s. Dark-haired and enigmatic, she broke the mold of platinum-blonde stereotypes—but was nonetheless typecast as an alluring femme fatale in most of her roles.

Hedy's off-screen personality couldn't have been more different. After moving from her native Austria to America in 1937, she lived quietly in the Hollywood Hills with her Great Dane, Donner, and spent much of her spare time exploring her true passion—inventing.

Most notably, during World War II, Hedy developed a technique called "frequency hopping," alongside her friend and neighbor, George Antheil. This allowed US and British torpedoes to strike their targets without being thwarted by a radio-jamming technique used by the Nazis. Their incredible invention later paved the way for the technologies behind modern-day Bluetooth and Wi-Fi.

Hedy's loyal Great Dane was by her side while she developed her inventions. In fact, Donner even inspired some of her work! In the 1940s, Hedy created the first-ever fluorescent dog collar so she could keep an eye on her beloved pooch when he was let into the garden at night.

Dogs were there for Hedy during her toughest times as well as her most creative moments. While Hedy later lived a reclusive life, she was never without the love and support of her canine best friends.

She lived quietly in the Hollywood Hills with her Great Dane, Donner.

"My little dog —
a heartbeat
at my feet."

- Edith Wharton

MICHELLE OBAMA

— LAWYER, AUTHOR & FORMER FIRST LADY —

On November 4, 2008, Barack and Michelle Obama made history when they became the first African American President and First Lady of the United States. After a successful career in law and public service, Michelle was eager to get to work on causes that were close to her heart—empowering girls through education, promoting poverty awareness, and advocating healthy eating. Also high on the agenda? Getting a dog.

During the grueling election, Michelle and Barack had promised their young daughters that, once the campaign was over, they would welcome a four-legged friend into the family. Three months after moving into the White House, the Obamas adopted a black-and-white Portuguese water dog puppy named Bo. He was joined by Sunny, another Portie, in 2013.

"Bo was supposed to be a companion for the girls. We had no idea how much he would mean to us all."

As "First Dogs" of the USA, Bo and Sunny received constant fan mail and requests to make public appearances. The two fluffballs were so popular that they had their own monthly schedules, which were always carefully checked by First Dog Mom, Michelle.

As well as being doggie ambassadors for the White House, Bo and Sunny provided happiness and comfort when Michelle needed some downtime from her own packed schedule as First Lady. "They can sit on my lap, they sit on my chair, they cuddle with me," she described in a 2016 interview. Whenever her role felt overwhelming, Michelle knew that her cherished pooches always had her back.

ELIZABETH II

QUEEN

The longest-reigning monarch in British history, Queen Elizabeth II was known for her strong sense of duty and public service throughout her 70 years on the throne. She was also known for her devotion to a characterful and very British breed of dog—the Pembroke Welsh corgi.

Her love of the breed began in childhood. In 1933, when Elizabeth was seven years old, she and her sister Margaret were given a corgi puppy called Dookie. The mischievous pup stole the hearts of the young princesses, who spent their time walking and brushing him and reportedly fed him his meals by hand. Dookie was less popular with guests at the palace, as he had a habit of nipping their heels.

On her 18th birthday, Elizabeth was presented with a corgi of her own, named Susan. The princess and Susan became inseparable, with the plucky pooch sneaking inside Elizabeth's carriage on her wedding day. During her lifetime, Elizabeth owned over 30 corgis, many of which were descended from Susan, and was rarely seen without her pack of loyal pups at her heels.

As well as being an important part of her personal life, the Queen's corgis played a key role in her public persona. Her love of dogs was well-known and helped give the Queen a warm and accessible image. A naturally shy person, Elizabeth often involved her dogs in events and ceremonies to help put guests at ease and break the ice.

"My corgis are family."

LINDSEY VONN

OLYMPIC SKIER

Considered one of the greatest skiers ever, Lindsey Vonn first caught the skiing bug as a child and went on to have a record-breaking career. She was the first American woman to win an Olympic gold medal in downhill skiing and won eight World Cup titles.

Lindsey's love of skiing is matched only by her love of dogs. She currently has three adored pooches—a Cavalier King Charles spaniel called Lucy, a mixed breed called Leo, and a Belgian shepherd dog called Jade.

Dogs first came into Lindsey's life during the winter of 2014. Just weeks before the start of the Sochi Olympics, Lindsey suffered a knee injury and made the devastating decision to pull out of the competition. A few days later, she found Leo at a rescue center. The 9-month-old pup had been hit by a car and, as a result, was also suffering from a bad knee. It was love at first sight!

"I don't think about being in a hotel anymore. I always have someone who is excited to see me."

Lindsey has spoken openly about how lonely life on the road can be for a professional athlete—contending with the pressure of competing alongside traveling far from home for long spells at a time. In 2017, Lindsey decided she needed a pooch pal who was small enough to travel with her, and welcomed Lucy to her growing pack. Lucy accompanied Lindsey around the world during the last two years of her career, as well as tagging along for press interviews and TV appearances.

Lindsey retired from professional skiing in 2019 but is still regularly seen hitting the slopes in the company of her dogs. Even little Lucy loves feeling the powder beneath her paws!

BILLIE HOLIDAY

MUSICIAN

In 1929, a young Billie Holiday first stepped onto a stage in a Harlem nightclub and changed music forever. One of the greatest jazz singers of all time, Billie's deeply sensitive interpretation of lyrics could draw out the hidden depths of classic standards and bring a timelessness to new pieces. Her iconic version of "Strange Fruit" became one of the most influential protest songs of the 20th century and still resonates with listeners today.

Born in 1915, Billie grew up in Baltimore and had a very difficult childhood, but her life was transformed when, as a teenager, she heard the records of jazz legends Louis Armstrong and Bessie Smith. Inspired to follow in their footsteps, she found a job as a singer and soon developed her own groundbreaking and genre-defining style.

> **"As long as he heard her voice, he was happy."**

Just as music was a source of strength and inspiration for Billie, so too was her love of dogs. Billie shared her life with many canine friends, including a Great Dane and two tiny Chihuahuas, Pepe and Chiquita. But her most beloved pooch was a boxer named Mister.

Billie and Mister were almost never apart. The gruff-looking dog accompanied his mistress from nightclub to nightclub, patiently waiting backstage while she performed and keeping fans at a "polite distance" once her set was over. According to one of her bandmates, "Mister would sit backstage near to where he could hear Lady's voice. As long as he heard her voice, he was happy."

10 THINGS

YOU CAN LEARN FROM DOGS

Every woman featured in this book is inspiring in her own way, and from them you can learn lessons in compassion, determination, and bravery. But by the side of each amazing woman is an equally wonderful dog with their own life lessons to offer.

1. BE LOYAL

Loyalty is perhaps the greatest lesson that dogs teach us. From everyday acts to heroic feats, dogs are unwavering in their devotion to the people they hold dear. Cherish your pack as a dog would, and greet your loved ones with the same pure joy as your faithful pooch.

2. GET OUTDOORS

Did someone say "walk"? Dogs adore feeling the wind in their fur and the grass beneath their paws, and their enthusiasm for the great outdoors is supported by science. Studies have shown that spending time outdoors can improve your mood and reduce feelings of stress and anxiety. Take the leash and head outside!

3. BE YOURSELF

From snuggling up to their favorite human to careering goofily around the park at the mere sight of a squirrel, dogs aren't afraid to wear their hearts on their sleeves. Be more dog—release your inhibitions and let your true self shine.

4. LIVE IN THE MOMENT

It's dinner time? Amazing! I've found an old chip on the pavement? Score! Dogs don't dwell on the past or future—they relish life in the present. Take inspiration from your furry friend and seize the day.

5. BE PLAYFUL

Dogs are great believers in the power of play. They are always up for a game of fetch, can have hours of fun with the simplest of toys, and use play to build strong bonds with one another. Their spontaneity teaches us to embrace our silly sides and run after Frisbees with joyful abandon.

6. TAKE NAPS

Did you know that the average adult dog spends around 15 hours a day snoozing? Dogs make sure they get plenty of naps, so when they are awake they have boundless energy for playing and hanging out with their favorite people. Join your dog on the sofa and prioritize some essential chill time together.

7. ENJOY THE SIMPLE THINGS

From rolling joyously in a mud puddle to relishing a back scratch, dogs enjoy the simple things in life. When we have a busy routine, it can be hard to switch off, but taking time to enjoy life's small pleasures can greatly benefit our mental health. Start with the delight of being greeted by a happy, wagging tail. There's nothing better.

8. NEVER SAY NO TO A COOKIE

The simple act of sharing food was probably how humans and dogs first became friends thousands of years ago. Dogs understand the power of food in bringing loved ones together and building social bonds. Share the cookies with your co-workers during your next coffee break. And give your canine chum an extra treat for imparting this wise lesson.

9. BE KIND

Dogs are kindhearted souls who want to be everyone's friend. Whether they're softly resting their head on your lap or presenting a stranger with a cherished toy, dogs teach us about the importance of small acts of kindness and spreading joy to all.

10. LOVE UNCONDITIONALLY

The bond between dogs and us is ancient and incredibly special. Human friends may come and go in your life, but your dog's love is selfless, true, and knows no bounds. Love like your dog, and in turn make sure you cherish that pure canine love bestowed upon you.

"There are things you get from the silent, devoted companionship of a dog that you can get from no other source."

— Doris Day

FRIDA KAHLO

ARTIST

One of the most iconic artists of the 20th century, Frida Kahlo is known for her intense and introspective paintings, her powerful celebration of identity, and her love of animals.

In her early life, Frida was drawn to science rather than art, and intended to study medicine. This all changed when Frida was 18 and was involved in a bus accident that left her with life-changing injuries. It was during her slow recovery that Frida taught herself to paint, channeling her feelings of pain, as well as her fierce determination and passion, into her art.

Throughout her life, Frida drew inspiration from her many pets. Of the 143 paintings she created, 55 of them feature animals. Casa Azul, Frida's home in Mexico City, was filled with free-roaming animals, from monkeys and parrots to fawns and, of course, dogs. Frida's favorite breed was the Xoloitzcuintli, also known as the Mexican hairless dog. An ancient breed, Xolos were considered sacred by the Aztecs, who believed the dogs had magical healing properties and helped guide souls in the afterlife.

The dogs' roots were important to Frida, who celebrated her own Mexican heritage in her work. European colonizers had dismissed Xolos as strange-looking creatures, driving the breed to near extinction. Frida treasured the unique appearance of her precious hounds. Enigmatic, strong, and survivors against all odds, these one-of a kind canines were fitting companions for this extraordinary woman.

Frida treasured the unique appearance of her precious hounds.

HEIDI KLUM

MODEL

A supermodel needs a superdog! German American model and businesswoman Heidi Klum is a devoted pooch parent and has owned many dogs over the years, including Jack Russells and German shorthaired pointers. In 2019, she made room on her sofa for a doggie giant and welcomed an Irish wolfhound puppy named Anton to her pack.

Heidi's taste in dogs is as varied as her talents. Born in Germany in 1973, Heidi moved to America in her late teens and quickly established herself as one of the most in-demand cover models, appearing on magazines such as *Vogue*, *ELLE*, and *Marie Claire*.

Her breakthrough moment came when she was picked to be one of the original "Angels" for Victoria's Secret. Since then, Heidi's spread her wings into various business ventures, including designing clothing lines and launching her own perfume brand. In the 2000s, she took her career in another direction as a TV producer and host for *Project Runway*, as a host on *Germany's Next Top Model*, and, more recently, as a judge on *America's Got Talent*.

Heidi's taste in dogs is as varied as her talents.

When she's not on TV, Heidi can be found chilling out with her beloved fur babies and working on her art. She's an accomplished painter, and dogs have often inspired Heidi's work. Most notably, in 2002, she was one of 100 artists involved in a public art project to commemorate the brave work of search-and-rescue dogs.

DODIE SMITH

AUTHOR

No writer has got inside the head of a dog quite like Dodie Smith. In Dodie's best-known book, *The Hundred and One Dalmatians*, dogs are far superior characters to the human "pets" they share their home with—Mr. and Mrs. Dearly are much loved by their dogs but a bit useless in a crisis. To rescue their puppies (and 82 others) from the clutches of the evil Cruella de Vil, Pongo and Missis have to take matters into their own paws.

Dodie and Dalmatians will forever go hand in paw.

A lifelong animal lover, Dodie grew up in Manchester, UK, in a family of theater enthusiasts and studied acting at RADA before becoming a successful playwright in the 1930s. It wasn't until 1948 that she wrote her first novel, *I Capture the Castle*. Dreamt up while Dodie and her husband were living in California during World War II, the book was partially inspired by her feelings of homesickness and became an instant coming-of-age classic.

Dogs make frequent appearances in Dodie's writing. A snowy-white bull terrier called Heloise plays a supporting, yet significant, role in *I Capture the Castle*. But Dalmatians captured her imagination and heart the most.

Dodie first fell in love with these spotty dogs in 1934, when her husband surprised her with a Dalmatian puppy as a 38th birthday present. When one of Dodie's friends came to meet the pup (named Pongo, of course) and joked that "He would make a nice fur coat," the idea for Dodie's classic tale was born. A book about bravery and the brilliance of dogs, it remains one of the best-loved children's books to this day. Dodie and Dalmatians will forever go hand in paw.

FURRY FLOWCHART

Take this test to find out which dog breed would be your perfect pooch. Read all about your canine personality in more detail on the next page.

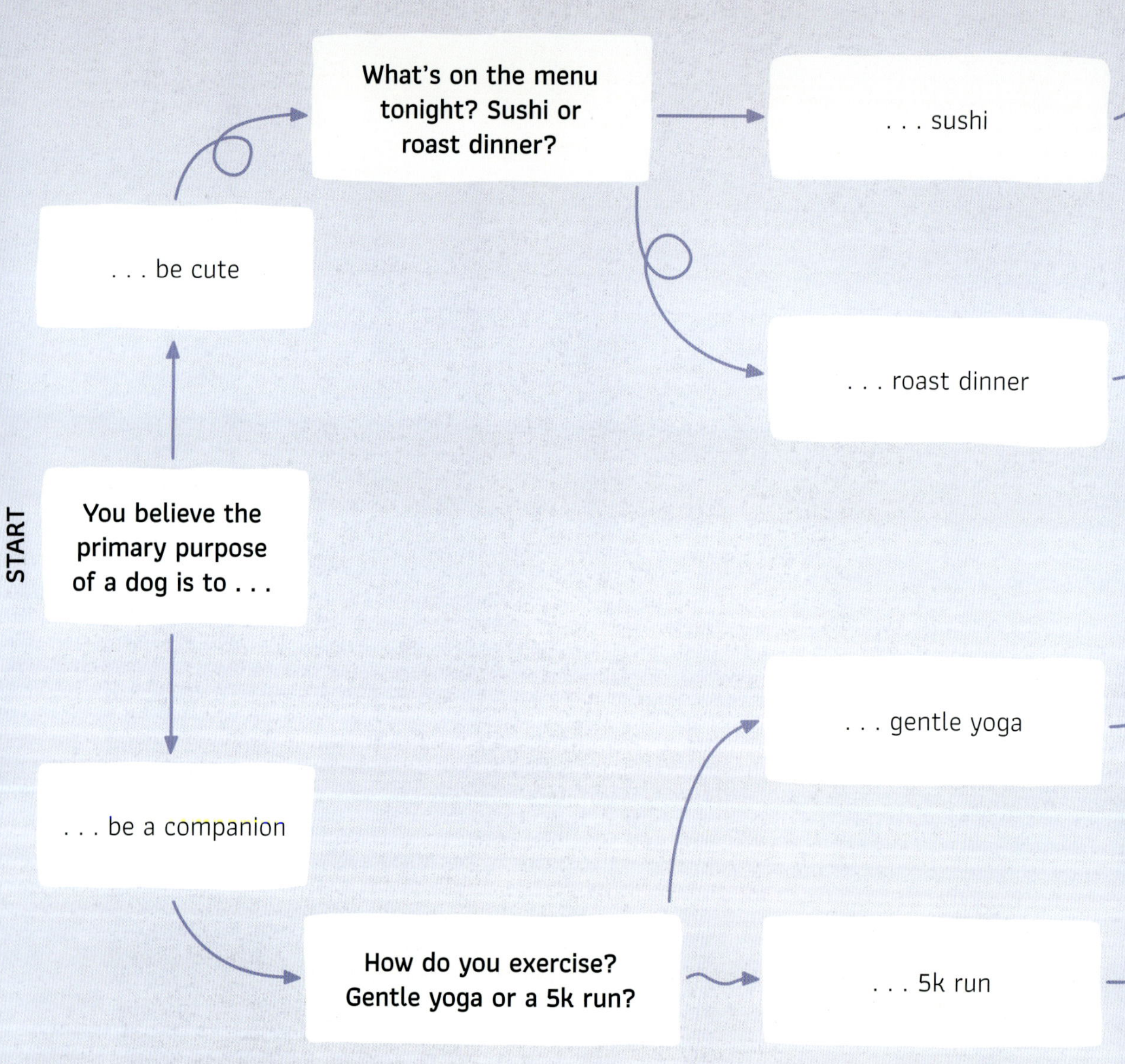

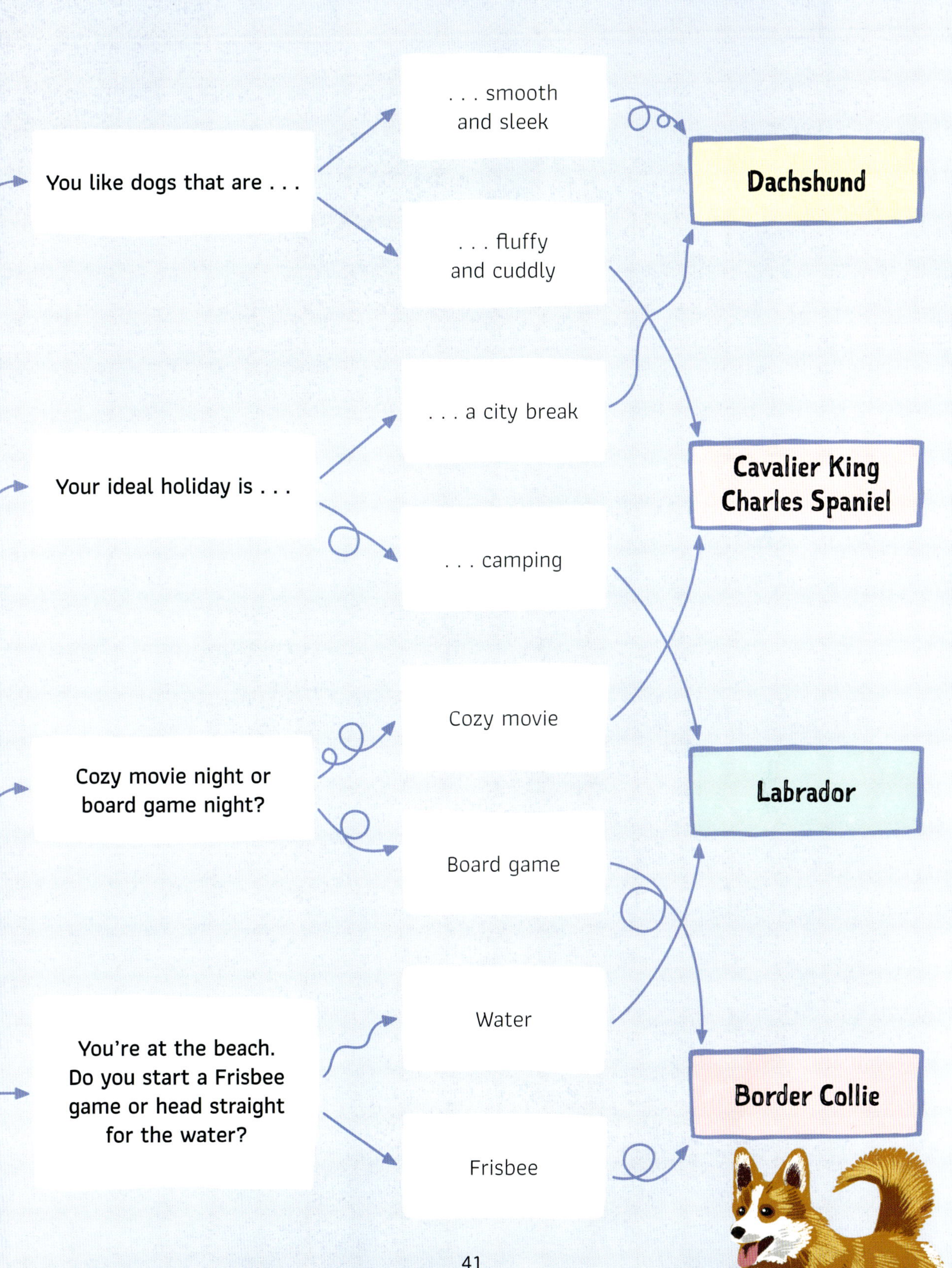
You like dogs that are . . .
. . . smooth and sleek
. . . fluffy and cuddly
Dachshund
Your ideal holiday is . . .
. . . a city break
. . . camping
Cavalier King Charles Spaniel
Cozy movie night or board game night?
Cozy movie
Board game
Labrador
You're at the beach. Do you start a Frisbee game or head straight for the water?
Water
Frisbee
Border Collie

FURRY FLOWCHART:
YOUR CANINE COMRADE

Discover the personality behind your paw-fect pooch.

— DACHSHUND —

Like to stand out from the crowd? You're a dachshund. These unmistakable canines were first bred in Germany to hunt badgers in underground tunnels ["dachshund" means "badger dog" in German]. They may seem small and comical, but don't underestimate the dachshund—these feisty pooches have the personality [and bark!] of a big dog. Dachshunds know their own minds and make lively, lovable partners in crime. Don't be afraid to be a dachshund in a park full of poodles.

— CAVALIER KING CHARLES SPANIEL —

Do you have hair as soft as silk and meltingly soulful eyes? Then your doggie doppelganger is the Cavalier King Charles spaniel. Cavies were originally bred to be lapdogs and their favorite place to be is with their adored human. Despite their regal bearing, Cavies are adaptable souls who are just as partial to a muddy frolic in the park as a cuddle on the sofa. With your friendly, easygoing nature, you'll find a kindred spirit in this sweet-natured dog.

— LABRADOR —

Your pooch pal is the Labrador. These outgoing dogs were originally bred in Newfoundland in Canada, where they were trained to fetch fishermen's nets from the sea. You're also a bit of a water baby and love being outdoors . . . whatever the weather! Intelligent, gentle, and loyal, Labradors make wonderful pets as well as assistance and guide dogs. Just like a Lab, you're a friend to everyone and are utterly devoted to your family pack.

— BORDER COLLIE —

Your paw-fect pairing is the border collie. Bred to herd sheep on the Scottish border, collies are some of the nimblest and smartest dogs on the planet. These canine Einsteins are happiest when they have a job to do, whether that's rounding things up or running around an agility course. While collies can seem intense, they have a softer, sensitive side and build immensely strong bonds with their favorite people. Like your canine counterpart, you care passionately about everything you do and love those closest to you deeply.

GLORIA ESTEFAN

MUSICIAN

Cuban American music legend Gloria Estefan shot to fame in the 1980s with a series of mega hits including "1-2-3," "Turn the Beat Around," and "Conga." With over 100 million record sales worldwide, eight Grammys, a Presidential Medal of Freedom, and a place in the Songwriters Hall of Fame, Gloria is one of the most successful female singers of all time.

When this conga queen isn't writing songs, appearing in films, performing on Broadway, or overseeing her business empire, she's probably having some well-earned chill time with her pack of beloved pooches.

Gloria is a great animal lover and has owned dogs throughout her life—at one point, she had nine! She is a particular fan of English bulldogs. Her brown-and-white bulldog, Noelle, even inspired Gloria to pen a series of children's books in the 2000s, which explored themes of not fitting in and overcoming obstacles.

Since her bulldogs passed away in 2012, Gloria has become a passionate advocate for adopting dogs from rescue centers and responsible pet ownership. As Gloria puts it, "Dogs offer unconditional love. They are such a wonderful gift, but also a responsibility that demands purposeful consideration."

When this conga queen isn't writing songs . . . she's probably having some well-earned chill time with her pack of beloved pooches.

MARILYN MONROE

ACTOR

In the 1953 film *Gentlemen Prefer Blondes*, Marilyn Monroe famously sings that "diamonds are a girl's best friend." Yet, the true rocks in Marilyn's life weren't diamonds at all—they were dogs.

> **"Dogs never bite me. Just humans."**

Marilyn Monroe was born Norma Jeane Mortenson in Los Angeles in 1926. At a young age, she was taken into care and spent her childhood in twelve foster homes. Shuffled between families, the little girl was drawn to the dependability of dogs. Her first dog was Tippy, a black-and-white crossbreed, who followed Marilyn to school and would sit outside until playtime so he could be with her. For Marilyn, dogs were a constant when adults were not.

In the 1950s, Marilyn quickly gained recognition for roles in *All About Eve* and *The Asphalt Jungle*. Her performances in *Gentlemen Prefer Blondes*, *How to Marry a Millionaire*, and, later, *Some Like It Hot*, cemented her status as a gifted actor and comedian, as well as a global superstar. Yet Marilyn struggled to gain respect from an industry that typecast her as a "blonde bombshell." Far from being "dumb," as her early film roles suggested, Marilyn took her profession extremely seriously, studying at the Actors Studio in New York, and was a voracious reader, an advocate for civil rights, and an active participant in politics.

In 1960, Frank Sinatra presented Marilyn with a Maltese terrier, whom she christened Maf. The little white dog was her constant companion in the last years of her life, sleeping on a fur coat and accompanying his mistress wherever she went. In contrast to Marilyn's troubled relationship with Hollywood, her relationship with dogs was always one of love and mutual respect. As Marilyn once put it, "Dogs never bite me. Just humans."

HELEN KELLER

ACTIVIST & AUTHOR

In 1882, when Helen Keller was 19 months old, she caught an unidentified illness that left her deaf and blind. Despite this, Helen learned to read, write, and speak with the help of her governess, Anne Sullivan, and later went on to gain a degree from Radcliffe College at Harvard University. A trailblazing educator, writer, and civil rights supporter, Helen worked for the American Foundation of the Blind for over 40 years, and toured the world to advocate for the deaf and blind communities.

From early childhood, dogs played an immensely important role in Helen's extraordinary life. She may not have been able to see or hear her dogs, but she could feel their steadfast presence beside her, the gentle weight of a paw on her lap, and the happy thump of a tail when she entered a room.

Dogs were never far from Helen's side. One of her most well-known companions was a Boston terrier called Phiz, who was gifted to Helen by her classmates at university. In later life, she helped introduce the Akita breed to America, after being presented with a dog during a lecture tour of Japan.

> ***"I am sure that I shall feel the touch of a cold nose and the wag of a tail in any world I go to."***

Helen expressed her deep love of dogs in an essay written in 1933. Reflecting on the things she would do first if she suddenly had vision, Helen wrote, "I should like to look into the loyal, trusting eyes of my dogs [. . .] whose warm, tender, and playful friendships are so comforting to me." To Helen, dogs were the ultimate best friend.

EMILY DICKINSON

POET

Emily Dickinson is one of the most important figures in the history of American poetry. Yet just ten of her nearly 1,800 poems were published while she was alive. The scale and stunning unconventionality of Emily's work were only discovered after her death in 1886, and her poems were not published in their entirety [and in the form she intended] until 1955.

Emily spent most of her life in the town of Amherst, Massachusetts. She loved going on long walks in the local countryside, and in 1849 her father presented her with a brown Newfoundland puppy to keep her company. Emily named her pup Carlo, and for the next 17 years, the big, bear-like dog was her steady shadow—or, as she put it, her "shaggy ally."

One of Emily's best-known poems begins as she must have started many mornings: "I started Early—Took my Dog." The line shows how Emily's walks with Carlo were a trigger for her poetic inspiration. From this everyday opener, Emily takes the reader on a transformative journey to the ocean, which is first a magical and then a stirring and unsettling place.

Spending most of her life in an inland town, Emily would never have walked all the way to the sea. But she was able to go there in her imagination, with Carlo by her side. Her poem explores themes of freedom and desire. It also speaks across the centuries of the liberating feeling of walking out into the wild with a furry friend at your heels.

"I started Early—Took my Dog—
And visited the Sea—
The Mermaids in the Basement
Came out to look at me—"

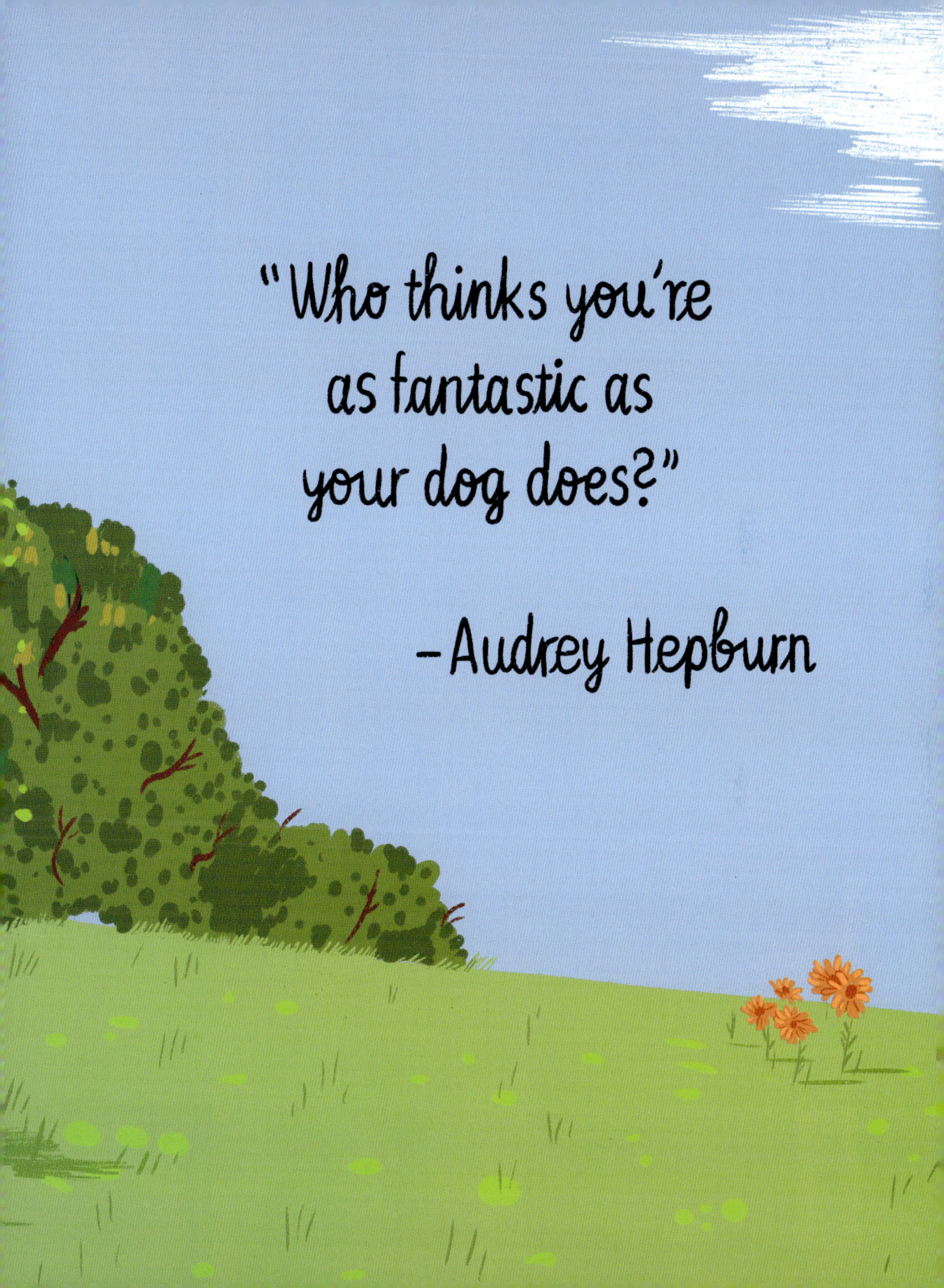
"Who thinks you're
as fantastic as
your dog does?"
–Audrey Hepburn

JANE GOODALL

— PRIMATOLOGIST & CONSERVATIONIST —

You may wonder what Jane Goodall, the world's leading expert on chimpanzees, is doing in a book about dogs. Well, despite having studied primates for the past 70 years, Jane has admitted that her favorite animal isn't a chimp . . .

If Jane's decision to travel to Tanzania in the late 1950s and make her mark in the world of primatology, then a male-dominated field, wasn't bold enough, her approach to studying animal behavior was revolutionary. Rather than observe chimps from a distance, Jane lived among them and made discoveries that transformed our understanding of our closest animal relatives. She proved that chimps make and use tools and display advanced social and emotional behaviors. Key to Jane's approach was her practice of naming the chimps that she studied; they were not just animals, but individuals.

"I had a wonderful teacher of animal behavior— my dog, Rusty."

It's quite possible that Jane wouldn't have embarked on her groundbreaking work if, years earlier, she hadn't met a very special dog. When Jane was a teenager, she started walking a neighbor's dog. Despite Jane's best efforts to teach the dog tricks, he couldn't understand even a simple "shake paw." But another local pooch, Rusty, often tagged along, too. One day, Rusty, who had been quietly watching the pair, reached out his paw to "shake" Jane's hand. This simple action sparked Jane's lifelong fascination with how animals think and their relationships with humans. Jane adopted Rusty and the pair became inseparable.

Jane has credited her close bond with Rusty as the inspiration behind her life's work: "I had a wonderful teacher of animal behavior—my dog, Rusty. He taught me that animals have personalities, minds, and feelings."

SALLY RIDE

ASTRONAUT

On June 18, 1983, Sally Ride smashed the highest glass ceiling possible when she became the first American woman—and third woman ever—to go into space. Back on solid ground, Sally devoted the rest of her life to championing equality and inspiring young people to achieve their potential.

Sally was supported on her journey into the history books by her family and her childhood companion—a rough collie called Tsigane. Tsigane arrived in the Ride family in 1961. Ten-year-old Sally dismissed her dad's unimaginative attempts to call their new pet "Lassie" and picked the dog's unusual name herself. It was inspired by a dog called "Tsigo," who Sally and her sister had encountered on a family trip to Eastern Europe—he had made a great impression on the girls by catching snowballs in his mouth.

Tsigane became Sally's adored playmate. The gentle collie would patiently watch over Sally while she did her homework each night and curl up to sleep beside her at lights out. She was probably by Sally's side when, in 1969, the future space scientist stayed up late to watch Neil Armstrong take his first steps on the Moon.

Just as watching a dog catch snowballs had fired Sally's imagination as a child, so her life's work became about encouraging girls to grab opportunities and reach for the stars. After leaving NASA in 1987, Sally co-founded a company with her life partner, Tam O'Shaughnessy, to encourage children to get into science. Away from the spotlight, Sally enjoyed a quiet life with Tam and their many beloved dogs.

Sally was supported on her journey into the history books by a rough collie called Tsigane.

BLACKPINK

MUSICIANS

Since their debut in 2016, K-pop sensation BLACKPINK has been smashing world records, raking in countless awards and accolades, and surfing the peak of the "Korean Wave" that has taken the world by storm. But if you're a true BLINK, you'll know that when Jennie, Jisoo, Rosé, and Lisa aren't making chart-topping tunes, they're hanging out with their pampered dogs. Meet Poochpink . . .

Jennie grew up with an adored spaniel called Kai and currently shares her life with Kuma, a brown Pomeranian. Kuma is firm friends with Jisoo's Maltese dog, Dalgom. Like all the BLACKPINK fur babies, Dalgom has expensive tastes and was once gifted a personalized bag from Dior!

> **"He gives me strength and is a very strong support."**

Animal-lover Rosé is the proud dog mom of a terrier called Hank, who she adopted from a rescue center in 2020. The pair are incredibly close, and Rosé often shows off the tricks she and Hank have mastered together. Lisa, meanwhile, bucked the BLACKPINK trend by welcoming a larger dog, a Doberman called Love, to her menagerie in 2021.

BLACKPINK's dogs are almost as famous as their owners, with each pooch garnering millions of followers on their social media accounts. Most importantly, however, they provide comfort away from the spotlight. In an interview with *Vogue Korea*, Jennie described how the experience of caring for Kuma has changed her life, making her feel "responsible for the first time." Like all of the band's pets, Kuma's steady presence provides welcome relief to Jennie's star-studded life on stage. As Jennie says, "He gives me strength and is a very strong support."

PRIYANKA CHOPRA JONAS

ACTOR & PRODUCER

Born in India in 1982, Priyanka Chopra dreamed of studying aeronautical engineering when, aged just 18, she won Miss World. This catapulted her to stardom in her home country, and offers for film work soon followed. By the 2010s, Priyanka had swapped Bollywood for Hollywood, and was well on her way to becoming a global icon. Alongside her film and entrepreneurial work, Priyanka supports numerous philanthropic causes and is especially passionate about women's and children's rights.

Never far from Priyanka's side—and usually seen tucked under her arm—is her Chihuahua-terrier cross, Diana. Diana came into Priyanka's life exactly when she needed her. In 2016, Priyanka had relocated to New York from India and was feeling isolated and lonely. Then she met a tiny puppy who had been rescued from the streets of Atlanta by an animal charity. Their bond was immediate and Priyanka has reflected on how much adopting Diana meant to her: "With Diana, I had somebody to take care of and, in return, she took care of me. If you look after them [dogs], they really look after you; they heal your heart."

"With Diana, I had somebody to take care of and, in return, she took care of me."

Ever since, the pair has been inseparable. Diana accompanies Priyanka to film sets, premieres, magazine shoots, and interviews, often sporting an outfit to match her mom's. Their pack has also grown. In 2018, Priyanka married musician Nick Jonas and they now live in LA with their daughter and two more dogs, Gino, a German shepherd, and Panda, a husky-Australian shepherd cross. An extra-special spot is always reserved on the sofa for Diana, though.

FURRY FACTS

Dogs are smart . . . and collies are top of the class.
The average dog can learn over 100 words and hand gestures, putting their intelligence on a par with a 2-year-old human. In studies of dog intelligence, border collies usually get full marks. A collie called Chaser from South Carolina was dubbed "the smartest dog in the world" after learning the names of over 1,000 toys!

Your dog could be right- or left-pawed.
Studies have shown that our furry friends have a preference for which paw they use. To find out whether your dog is right- or left-pawed, present them with a toy or tasty treat and see which paw they use to interact with you.

A breed of dog called the basenji doesn't bark . . .
. . . it yodels! Yes, you read that right, this African breed has a voice box that's shaped in a different way than that of other dogs, so it makes its feelings known with a one-of-a-kind howl.

A dog's nose print is as unique as your fingerprint.
Some phone apps have even been developed to find missing dogs using their nose prints. The idea is that you can scan a lost dog's nose and, if they are registered on the app, see instantly whether they have been reported as missing. Sounds paw-some to us!

Chow chows have black-blue tongues.
According to Chinese legend, the breed got its unusual tongue color when a curious dog licked the sky as it was being painted.

Dogs dream.
All dogs dream when they sleep—you've probably noticed your doggie pal's paws twitching while they snooze. Scientific evidence suggests that smaller dogs dream a lot, but have quite short dreams. Bigger dogs dream less frequently, but tend to have longer dreams.

Dogs have a SUPER sense of smell.
The average dog has 100 million scent receptors in its nose (compare that to your mere 5 million!). Bloodhounds have a whopping 300 million scent receptors—in fact, their sense of smell is so on the money that it can be used as evidence in some US courts.

The saluki is one of the oldest breeds of dog in the world.
These elegant hounds have stood by our side for at least 5,000 years. Images of slender dogs with long, feathery ears have been found carved on ancient Egyptian tombs and mosaics across the Middle East.

Dogs have a calming effect on us.
Research has shown that simply petting a dog can help lower our stress levels. It works the other way, too—when a dog is gently stroked by their human, their heart rate is lowered and they feel calmer.

MARY ANNING

PALEONTOLOGIST

If you'd taken a walk along the shore at Lyme Regis, Dorset, in the 1820s, chances are you would have crossed paths with Mary Anning. Mary was a self-taught paleontologist who lived in Lyme Regis all her life, and spent her days unearthing the secrets hidden in its limestone cliffs.

Known today as the "Jurassic Coast," this area of southern England is the only place in the world where rocks from the Triassic, Jurassic, and Cretaceous periods can be seen in one place, and it is bursting with the fossilized remains of ancient creatures.

She may have been shunned by her peers, but Mary could always count on her dog, Tray.

Mary's incredible finds included the first *Ichthyosaurus* fossil, the first complete *Plesiosaurus*, and Britain's first *Pterodactylus*. Her work transformed the Victorians' understanding of the prehistoric world. The Geological Society discussed her discoveries and male scientists sought her advice. Yet Mary, as a woman, a nonconformist, and a member of the working class, was excluded from debates and her contributions to research were often uncredited.

She may have been shunned by her peers, but Mary could always count on her dog, Tray. With his feathery ears flapping in the wind, Tray kept Mary company as she painstakingly uncovered her fossils. The fact that Tray appears in the only known portrait of Mary shows just how much his companionship meant to her.

Mary is now recognized as a pioneering scientist and her legacy lives on in the fossils she found. So too does her relationship with Tray. If you visit Lyme Regis today, you can see a statue that shows Mary striding toward the beach, her best friend forever trotting faithfully at her heels.

MARIA CALLAS

OPERA SINGER

Powerful, passionate, and devoted to her craft, Maria Callas was one of the most iconic opera singers of the 20th century. Maria's unique soprano voice combined with her impressive acting talent allowed her to transcend the world of opera and break into the mainstream in the 1950s and '60s. To this day, she remains the best-selling classical singer of all time.

Born in New York in 1923 to Greek parents, Maria showed an interest in singing from an early age. She spent her teenage years in Athens, where she was classically trained, before making her name with a string of phenomenal performances in Italy in the 1940s.

Maria's story is often overshadowed by her highly publicized relationship with the tycoon Aristotle Onassis. A truer reflection of this extraordinary woman is her relationship with her dogs; "Only my dogs will not betray me," she once reflected.

Maria had a soft spot for miniature poodles. Her first was named Toy, and he was succeeded by a pair called Pixie and Djedda. Just like their mistress, these adored dogs were fiery, faithful, and impeccably stylish. The poodles accompanied Maria on tour, slept at the foot of her bed, and Maria herself combed their curly fur to paw-fection. Perhaps unsurprisingly for a prima donna's pooches, they also enjoyed making their voices heard. In an interview from 1968, little Djedda is recorded howling alongside Maria as she warms up!

Just like their mistress, these adored dogs were fiery, faithful, and impeccably stylish.

CANINE HALL OF FAME

POCKET-SIZED POOCH

The shortest dog in the world at the moment is a teeny-tiny Chihuahua called Pearl from Florida. Little Pearl is just 3.5 inches tall, roughly the height of a teacup!

GENTLE GIANT

The tallest dog ever recorded was a Great Dane called Zeus from Michigan. This gentle giant measured 39 inches when standing on his four paws and 88 inches if he stood up on his hind legs!

GOLDEN OLDIE

The oldest dog ever was a female Australian cattle dog called Bluey. She was born in 1910 and lived for an astonishing 29 years and 5 months. Her owners claimed that Bluey worked on the farm rounding up cattle and sheep for 20 of those years.

TOP TRICKS

Two dogs hold the record for "most tricks performed in one minute by a dog." An Australian shepherd dog called Daiquiri and a border collie named Hero both performed an incredible 60 tricks in 60 seconds.

FASTEST DOG

Slim and streamlined, sighthounds are easily the quickest dogs in the park. Greyhounds are the fastest dogs of all, clocking up a top speed of 45 miles per hour.

SKATER DOG

While some dogs rely on their paws for speed, others have more creative ways of getting about. Tillman was an English bulldog who enjoyed riding around his California home on a skateboard. In 2009, he set the record for "fastest 100 meters on a skateboard by a dog," scooting over the finish line in 19.678 seconds.

HERO DOGS

In 1943, the PDSA Dickin Medal was set up to recognize the work of animals in World War II. It has been awarded over 75 times since then for acts of incredible bravery and devotion. To date, 38 dogs have received this honor.

OPEN WIDE!

In 2020, a golden retriever called Finley set a world record for "most tennis balls held in a dog's mouth" when he picked up six tennis balls! Finley hasn't let fame go to his head and still enjoys playing fetch and chasing squirrels that wander into his backyard.

FLORENCE KNOLL

ARCHITECT

Florence Knoll was one of the most radical designers of the mid-20th century. Alongside her business partner and husband, Hans Knoll, she established a company that pioneered modernist design in the 1950s. Florence has also been credited with revolutionizing the workspace, creating offices that were open-plan and practical for workers. If Florence's functional designs feel familiar now, that shows just how influential she was and continues to be.

A shaggy Old English sheepdog may seem an unusual choice for a designer known for her crisp, clean lines. Yet Cartree, Florence's cherished pooch, was never far from her side while she developed her designs. Despite their stunning looks, Old English sheepdogs were originally bred to do a hard day's work herding cattle and sheep. Perhaps this was part of the breed's appeal to Florence, who sought to combine style and practicality in her own work.

As well as accompanying Florence to her office, Cartree became an unofficial mascot for the Knoll company, appearing in catalogs and advertisements. His cuddly appearance and gentle character offset Florence's geometric designs and brought a friendliness to her modernist brand.

A shaggy Old English sheepdog may seem an unusual choice for a designer known for her crisp, clean lines.

Ultimately, Florence wanted the buildings and interiors she designed to be accessible and enjoyed by all—including four-legged family members. Together, this groundbreaking woman and her furry best friend changed the spaces we live in for the better.

CHLOÉ ZHAO

DIRECTOR

In April 2021, Chloé Zhao lifted the Oscar for Best Director and made history as the first Asian woman [and the second woman ever] to win in that category. Chloé was collecting the award for her work on *Nomadland*, which tells the story of a woman forced to leave her home and embark on a journey across America in her camper van. Acclaimed for its compassion and beauty, the film has become a modern-day classic and cemented Chloé's reputation as one of the world's most important filmmakers.

What better way to wrap up a busy day of filming than to come home to a happy, waggy tail?

Chloé has a nomadic soul herself. Born in Beijing, China, in 1982, she was drawn to cinema from a young age. After spending time at schools in the UK and Los Angeles, Chloé studied film at university in New York. Her first two feature films, *Songs My Brothers Taught Me* [2015] and *The Rider* [2017], established her as a talent to watch.

When Chloé isn't making award-winning films, she embraces a quiet life in the Californian mountains with her partner and two dogs—Taco, a crossbreed, and Rooster, a collie. Both dogs have very different personalities: Taco is older and mellower, while Rooster is young and energetic—a bit like Chloé's movies!

Chloé thrives on making films that span a myriad of genres, from Marvel epics to Shakespearean biopics. In fact, she often tries to have a smaller project on the go at the same time as a bigger movie because each film "keeps the other in check." And what better way to wrap up a busy day of filming than to come home to a happy, waggy tail? Or maybe an excitable spin, in Rooster's case.

ALEXIA PUTELLAS

SOCCER PLAYER

In the last decade, women's soccer has conquered the world, and Spanish midfielder Alexia Putellas has been a star player in its story. Regarded as one of the greatest soccer players of her generation, Alexia has championed the women's game throughout her career and, as captain, led the Spanish women's team in their World Cup win in 2023.

In 2012, aged 18, Alexia signed with Barcelona FC—the club she had supported since childhood. In the years since, she has helped her team win numerous trophies, including the UEFA Women's Champions League. As an individual player, she's won the prestigious Ballon d'Or twice and the UEFA Women's Player of the Year [also twice!], to name just two.

Alexia has recalled how, as a child, she would go everywhere with a soccer ball tucked under one arm. As an adult, she's made room for a soccer ball-sized pooch under the other. Nala the Pomeranian was Alexia's proudest supporter on her path to World Cup glory. Off the field, the athlete was seldom seen without her furry pal, with Nala accompanying Alexia to award ceremonies and photoshoots as well as enjoying holidays and hikes together.

Alexia credited her beloved dog with supporting her mental health during highs and lows. In an interview in 2022, she described their special bond: "That company, it's something we may easily take for granted but it's so important [. . .] to have a connection like that."

Nala the Pomeranian was Alexia's proudest supporter on her path to World Cup glory.

JENNIFER ANISTON

ACTOR

"I'll be there for you . . ." states the iconic theme song to smash-hit sitcom *Friends*, which catapulted Jennifer Aniston to superstardom in the 1990s. But the gang better make room on that orange sofa, because Jen's BFFs are of the four-legged variety. "My dog friends are very special," she reflected in a 2019 interview. "They don't text or buy me flowers, but they do so much more. They pick me up when I need it, they always greet me when I come home, and they never complain about anything."

Friends established Jennifer as one of the world's best-loved actors and, since the show ended in 2004, she has enjoyed a successful film career, ranging from romantic comedies to hard-hitting dramas. One of the highest paid actors in the world, Jennifer shares her wealth with numerous charities and causes, supporting children's hospitals, campaigning for LGBTQ+ rights, and donating to humanitarian causes.

She is also a lifelong advocate of rescue pets and has adopted many much-loved dogs from animal shelters over the years—notably Dolly, a white German shepherd, and Norman, a corgi-terrier cross.

"The most unconditional form of love you can encounter is with a dog. They're loyal and they're always, always faithful."

Her current pack includes Clyde, a schnauzer mix; Sophie, a black-and-white pitbull cross; and Lord Chesterfield, a Labrador cross. Little Clyde—the most portable of her trio—regularly accompanies Jennifer to work on her hit drama series *The Morning Show*. Jennifer has always counted dogs as her friends and knows that her furry family will always be there for her.

"I want to work like a dog, doing what I
was born to do with joy and purpose.

I want to play like a dog,
with total, jolly abandon.

I want to love like a dog,
with unabashed devotion ...

The fact that we still live with dogs,
even when we don't have to herd or
hunt our dinner, gives me hope for
humans and canines alike."

– Oprah Winfrey

SERENA WILLIAMS

TENNIS CHAMPION

One of the greatest athletes of all time, Serena Williams has been shattering records and transforming the world of tennis since she first stepped onto a professional court in the 1990s. Alongside her sister, Venus, Serena has revolutionized the women's game with her powerful playing style. The winner of 23 Grand Slam titles—more than any other player—Serena also shares 14 Grand Slam doubles titles with Venus and three Olympic golds.

In 1999, just two weeks before Serena's first Grand Slam victory, a furry friend joined the Williams family. Named Jackie Pete (in honor of tennis legend Pete Sampras), the little Jack Russell pup was Serena's constant companion for the next 16 years. Jackie was soon joined by a Maltese named Laurelei, and together the doggie duo accompanied Serena to tournaments all over the world.

Reaching the heights of professional tennis and staying there for over 20 years is not easy, and Serena faced challenges on and off the court during her career. Throughout it all, she could always count on her dogs to provide kindness, joy, and comfort.

"Chip is my most loyal fan. At every Grand Slam, he's there supporting me."

Serena's current top dog is a Yorkshire terrier named Chip (full name Christopher "Chip" Rafael Nadal). In the last few years of Serena's professional career, little Chip could often be seen showing his support from the sidelines or giving his fur mom a cuddle before she started a match. As you'd expect from the dog of a tennis legend, Chip is also said to be an ace at fetch!

DOROTHY PARKER

WRITER

"Four-legged people—but nicer," is how American writer and critic Dorothy Parker described her furry best friends. Famed for her razor-sharp wit, Dorothy showed her softer side when it came to dogs.

Dorothy shared her life with an incredible cast of pooches—from Boston terriers and boxers to Dalmatians and crossbreeds. Her muttley crew included a black poodle called Cliché (so named because "the streets are carpeted with black poodles") and a black-and-tan dachshund called Robinson. Little Robinson was gifted to Dorothy during a visit to Munich, Germany, and he became her closest ally back in New York, perching proudly on Dorothy's lap as she held court at high-society parties and literary soirées.

Famed for her razor-sharp wit, Dorothy showed her softer side when it came to dogs.

Dorothy was known as one of the most brilliant conversationalists of her time. Her caustic wit came to the fore in articles she wrote as an editor for *Vogue* and drama critic for *Vanity Fair*. Later on, it was sharpened further in her short stories for *The New Yorker*. The latter, in particular, helped to establish Dorothy as the voice of liberated 1920s women.

After leaving *Vanity Fair* in 1920 (the result, in part, of a particularly cutting drama review), Dorothy became a freelance writer and poet, and the founding member of the Algonquin Round Table, a literary society that brought together some of the brightest and best wordsmiths of the day. But Dorothy's favorite company was always of the four-legged variety: "I never had enough dogs in my life," she once reflected—and she'd owned at least 20.

ISABELLA ROSSELLINI

ACTOR & MODEL

It was perhaps inevitable that the daughter of two cinematic legends, Swedish actor Ingrid Bergman and Italian film director Roberto Rossellini, would herself become a cultural icon. After coming to prominence in the 1980s with roles in *White Nights* (1985) and *Blue Velvet* (1986), Isabella Rossellini became known as the ethereally beautiful muse of directors David Lynch and Martin Scorsese, and the longtime face of cosmetics brand Lancôme. But her first love wasn't film and fashion—it was animals.

Today, Isabella shares her organic farm on Long Island with a menagerie of dogs, bees, pigs, and chickens. Her journey from film star to farmer began in her 50s. After deciding to pursue her childhood fascination with animals, she enrolled at university and earned a master's degree in animal behavior and conservation. These studies have informed much of Isabella's film and theater work over the last decade, including *Green Porno*, a series of acclaimed short films about animal reproduction, and *Link Link Circus*, which saw the actor and her terrier, Pan, unpack the relationship between humans and animals live on stage.

Isabella's own pooches often share the sofa with guide dogs in training. For the last 20 years, the actor has been involved in the American Guide Dogs for the Blind Foundation. As well as being an ambassador for the Foundation's vital work, Isabella has helped to raise at least ten adorable guide dog puppies, preparing them for their future roles as the ultimate best friends.

Isabella's own pooches often share the sofa with guide dogs in training.

MARIE ANTOINETTE

QUEEN

Marie Antoinette will forever be associated with the decadence and frivolity that brought the French monarchy to destruction. Yet France's ill-fated, final queen was also one of history's greatest dog lovers.

Dogs were there for Marie throughout her life. When the princess first arrived at the French court of Versailles in 1770, as the bride of the king's eldest son, she was only 14 years old. Desperately missing the family she had left behind in Austria, Marie turned to her canine friends for comfort.

She requested that a pug be sent to keep her company. But not just any pug; it had to be a pug from her home city of Vienna. When the little dog eventually arrived, he joined a growing entourage of pooches that shadowed Marie through the gilded corridors of Versailles.

Depending on whose story you believe, dogs were also there for Marie at her infamous death. One legend tells how, when the queen was executed by guillotine, the silence was broken only by the sound of her beloved papillon, Coco, howling with grief. Another story claims that Coco was entrusted to Marie's children's governess before the queen died, and lived a long and peaceful life far away from the revolution.

Dogs were there for Marie throughout her life . . . and at her infamous death.

For much of history, Marie Antoinette has been painted as the villain, but in reality she was probably many complicated things. One truth that has survived the centuries is Marie's love and devotion to her canine confidantes.

MARLENE DIETRICH

ACTOR

No star has glittered quite like Marlene Dietrich. One of the most glamorous actors of the silver screen, Marlene was known for her intoxicating voice, androgynous beauty, and diverse portrayals of women. Openly bisexual, her gender-bending style and liberated values saw her become Hollywood's original LGBTQ+ icon.

Born in Germany in 1901, Marlene started her career as a chorus girl, immersing herself in the freewheeling nightclub culture of 1920s Berlin. Her role in *The Blue Angel* (1930), one of Germany's first talking films, made her name and fast-tracked her to Hollywood, where she would appear in a string of popular films in the 1930s. One of her most iconic scenes came in *Morocco* (1930), when she stunned audiences by appearing in a men's tailcoat and kissing her female co-star. She may have leant into her image as a sultry femme fatale, but nothing Marlene did was ever predictable.

An Afghan hound goes its own way, just like Marlene did.

Marlene became a US citizen in 1937, denounced Nazism, and poured her energy into helping the American war effort during World War II. She devoted much of her time and musical talents to aid the troops and raised money to help Jewish refugees.

At the peak of her career, Marlene owned several Afghan hounds, a stylish breed that became popular with Hollywood celebrities in the 1940s and '50s. These dogs were a particularly great match for Marlene—effortlessly glamorous, alluringly aloof, and with a look all of their own. An Afghan hound goes its own way, just like Marlene did.

HOW TO SPEAK DOG

Dogs are top of the class when it comes to understanding us—they are sensitive to our emotions, can read our expressions, and follow our hand gestures. But are you as good at speaking your dog's language? This handy guide will help you to understand what your canine companion is trying to tell you.

When your dog approaches you with its head held high, mouth open in a relaxed way, and tail wagging, they're telling you "I'm SO happy—especially now that you're here!"

A waggy tail is a happy dog's calling card. When a dog is content, they will usually wag their tail and have an all-round air of relaxation—such as a partly open, soft mouth, a gentle expression (which can look like a squint), and a confident stance. That said, pay close attention to the way a dog holds its tail. A slow wag normally means "I'm feeling relaxed," and a broad, faster wag, which sometimes spins the tail all the way round in a circle, means the dog is OVERJOYED. At the other end of the spectrum, a stiff tail suggests a dog is feeling alert, possibly a bit tense, while a tail tucked between their legs means a dog is feeling scared.

When your dog puts its chest on the ground, bottom in the air, and wiggles its tail, your dog is saying "This is so much fun! Play with meeeeee!!!"

While dogs use noises and smells to communicate with one another, they mainly use their bodies to tell their human friends how they're feeling. This posture, sometimes called a "play bow," is a dog's way of letting you know they are excited and playful. Dogs also use this pose to tell other dogs that they are friendly—a confident dog may use a play bow to tell a shyer dog they have nothing to worry about and to encourage them to join in the fun.

When your dog lies on the floor and rolls over, showing its tummy, your dog is saying "I trust you."

Many dogs love tummy rubs as a way of affirming their bond with their special human—if a dog lets you rub its belly, they really trust you. However, dogs also show their tummies as a sign of submission. It's important to be able to read when your dog is just after a good belly scratch and when they might be telling you something else. Dogs use submissive signals as a way of calming down a situation—for example, when a dog is meeting strangers (or new dogs) for the first time. By rolling on its back and showing its tummy, a vulnerable part of itself, a dog is trying to tell you that they are not a threat.

When a dog yawns, they are saying "Don't mind me!"

Some expressions—such as yawning—can be harder to read than others. A yawn can indicate sleepiness, but dogs yawn to calm themselves when they're feeling anxious, too—if they're waiting in a vet's office, for example. Dogs also use yawning as a nonthreatening signal to whoever or whatever is stressing them out. By yawning at an aggressive dog, for instance, your dog is saying "I'm indifferent to your barking and I'm not looking for a fight!"

"I think dogs are the most amazing creatures; they give unconditional love. For me they are the role model for being alive."

-Gilda Radner